2020:
WHAT A YEAR

CHRISTOPHER BONNER

AuthorHouse™
1663 Liberty Drive
Bloomington, IN 47403
www.authorhouse.com
Phone: 833-262-8899

Because of the dynamic nature of the Internet, any web addresses or links contained in this book may have changed since publication and may no longer be valid. The views expressed in this work are solely those of the author and do not necessarily reflect the views of the publisher, and the publisher hereby disclaims any responsibility for them.

Any people depicted in stock imagery provided by Getty Images are models, and such images are being used for illustrative purposes only.
Certain stock imagery © Getty Images.

This book is printed on acid-free paper.

ISBN: 978-1-6655-1495-8 (sc)
ISBN: 978-1-6655-1496-5 (e)

Library of Congress Control Number: 2021901377

Print information available on the last page.

Published by AuthorHouse 01/28/2021

authorHOUSE®

2020; What A Year

Twas the year 2020 and all over the
world; everybody was freightened;
every boy every girl

So many were nervous and others afraid,
for Covid 19 a pandemic had spread

Some people wore face shields and others wore masks. The children all wondered how long will this last?

There were no real answers, no one really knew. The whole world was in chaos, what on earth would we do?

Everything was shut down, all the stores had to close; financial crisis and hardship all quickly arose.

Then it got worse with sickness and dying,
Hospitals filled and so many families crying.

The Leaders tried to give solace and comfort our hearts; but that just wasn't enough for lives so torn apart

Even churches were suffering no
fellowship of love, for we couldn't come
together to gain peace from above

Thank goodness for livestream, technology
came through; for we could still have
church through social media groups

Through Spring and into the Summer, this pandemic still stayed; we couldn't seem to shake it, despite how much we prayed.

Vacations were cancelled, nations' borders were closed, no international travel for the threat that it posed

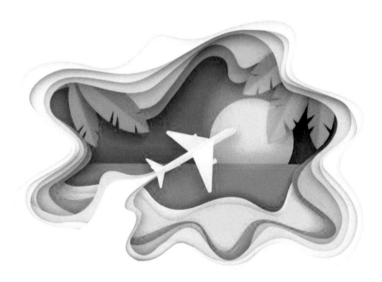

Planes were grounded, no one was
in flight; everyone was stuck in their
homes all day and all night

Summer has gone and fall has begun, but no
back to school stories of vacations in the sun

Most schools were still closed with
virtual learning, and parents upset
with their hearts all yearning

Get these kids back to school so we
get peace and quiet; home schooling
is hard, we cannot deny it

Things slowly reopened, jobs churches
and schools, just maybe we're getting back
to normal, now wouldn't that be cool

However, that was a small effort and
the benefits vague; as we still had a
ways to go to overcome this plague

Above all this, was a Presidential
election, the country was divided
on who was the best selection.

Biden was the winner at the end
of the day, though Trump couldn't
believe it, he suspected foul play

He voiced his concern and launched an
investigation, until finally accepting he
was no longer the leader of the nation

He packed up his things and exited the house,
to move on with his life along with his spouse.

Now the year is almost gone, and
Winter has replaced Fall; and you know
the most important question of all

Will there be Christmas, will Santa
Clause come; could he possibly
also be stuck in his home?

The children will be saddened their
hearts would be broken; to know there
would be no gifts for them to open

Even parents would grapple to face such
a demise; so thank goodness Christmas
would come and bring a surprise.

For the Officials' year long work
had not been in vain; they finally
developed a Covid 19 vaccine

What joy, what relief, and now we can cope;
for people can now once again rejoice in hope

Families began early, decorating with
trees and lights; and all over the world
hearts are again cheery and bright

And even before Christmas, the
vaccine it arose, about mid-December
they gave the first dose

First critical care workers received
vaccination, then in order, to
others all over the nations.

With great joy in our hearts, our ears can again listen; to hear "Now Dasher, now Dancer, now Prancer and Vixen"

Our eyes fixed to the sky as they twinkle and glisten; to see "Comet and Cupid, and Donder and Blitzen"

With Rudolph at lead with his shiny red nose; through a year full of gloominess, we're glad it still glows

With Santa at the reins, toys and gifts all in tow; he'll travel the world through rain, sleet, or snow.

As he visits our homes we can hear with delight; that wonderful phrase "Merry Christmas To All, and To All a Good Night"

Printed in the United States
By Bookmasters